A NEW FRONTIER

THE PAST, PRESENT, AND FUTURE OF THE SEARCH FOR EXTRATERRESTRIAL LIFE

NICKI PETER PETRIKOWSKI

ROSEN
PUBLISHING

NEW YORK

Published in 2016 by The Rosen Publishing Group, Inc.
29 East 21st Street, New York, NY 10010

First Edition

Library of Congress Cataloging-in-Publication Data

Petrikowski, Nicki Peter.
 A new frontier : the past, present, and future of the hunt for extraterrestrial life / Nicki Peter Petrikowski.
     pages cm. -- (The search for other Earths)
Audience: Grades 7-12.
Includes bibliographical references and index.
ISBN 978-1-4994-6296-8 (library bound)
1. Life on other planets. 2. Extraterrestrial beings. I. Title.
QB54.P525 2016
576.8'39--dc23
                           2015025515

Manufactured in China

CONTENTS

INTRODUCTION

One of the most profound questions humans have asked themselves for thousands of years is whether we are alone in the universe. Does life exist beyond Earth, or is our planet so special, the necessary circumstances so rare that only here life was able to develop?

Considering there are hundreds of billions of stars in our galaxy alone, with an estimated one hundred billion planets, it seems unlikely that Earth is unique in that respect. It has been thought for a long time that extraterrestrial life exists, but so far there has been no proof. Thanks to improving technology and increasing knowledge of the universe, an answer seems finally to be in reach. It has been discovered that there are more places where life could exist (or could have existed in the past) than previously thought, and the technology exists to examine them more closely and thoroughly than ever before.

Looking up at the Milky Way and its great amount of stars, it seems improbable that there should be life only in one place.

At a recent panel discussion, NASA chief scientist Ellen Stofan said that she expected to see strong indications of life beyond Earth within ten years time and definitive evidence in twenty to thirty years.

From the speculation of ancient philosophers to modern exobiology, the search for extraterrestrial life has come a long way. The past, present, and future of the search is described in this resource as the hunt seems to be approaching its end. But then the discovery of life beyond Earth would not really be an end but rather a beginning.

CHAPTER ONE

THE HISTORY OF EXTRATERRESTRIAL LIFE

The night sky full of stars is an awesome sight, and people have probably wondered what might be out there all throughout human history. While we have no way of knowing what our oldest ancestors thought about the possibility of life existing beyond Earth, written documents show that the topic of extraterrestrial life, which seems to be such a modern idea, was already a cause for debate two and a half millennia ago.

THOUGHTS ON EXTRATERRESTRIAL LIFE IN ANCIENT GREECE

Many ancient cultures, from China to Egypt to the Maya of Middle America, developed a basic understanding of astronomy. Through observation of the sky and the motions of the celestial

From time immemorial the impressive sight of the night sky has led people to wonder what is beyond Earth.

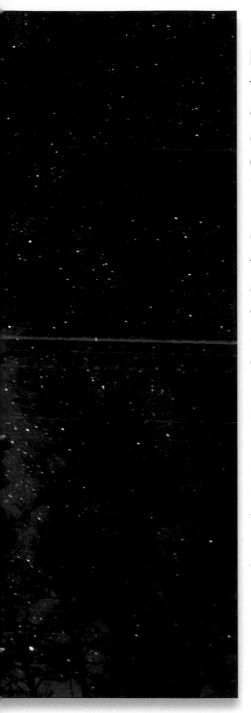

bodies that are visible to the naked eye, they were able to devise calendars and, in some cases, predict eclipses with astounding precision.

Philosophers in ancient Greece went a step further and started to wonder what the cosmos they were observing was made of and how it worked, without attributing natural phenomena to the actions of gods or other supernatural causes. Supporters of the school of thought called atomism believed that the cosmos consisted of tiny indestructible particles—atoms (from the Greek *atomos*, meaning "uncuttable" or "indivisible"). The first to come up with the idea (as far as we know) was Leucippus of Miletus in the fifth century BCE, and the concept was later refined by his pupil Democritus and others.

The atomists proposed that our world had been formed by chance through the random motion of atoms existing in infinite number, and as a consequence it stood to reason that other worlds had come into existence in the same way. And since there was life on Earth, they concluded that there had to be life in these other worlds as well.

Aristotle (384–322 BCE) did not believe in the plurality of worlds like the atomists did. He argued that the world was made of four elements (earth, water, air, and fire) and that the celestial realm consisted of a fifth element called quintessence or aether. Instead of the random motions of the atoms, he ascribed to each of the elements a characteristic motion, downward in the case of earth and water, upward for fire and air, and circular for aether.

From that he concluded that there could only be one world, because if there were more than

The Greek philosopher Aristotle was one of the most influential thinkers of all time, and his belief that Earth was unique was upheld for many centuries.

one, these motions would get mixed up. Earth in our world moves toward the center, but if there were another world, the element would have to move toward the center of that world as well, moving both downward and upward, which he, almost two thousand years before our modern concept of gravity was formulated, considered to be impossible. Hence Aristotle and his followers thought our world to be unique, which ruled out the existence of extraterrestrial life.

THE RISE OF CHRISTIANITY AND THE MIDDLE AGES

Christianity rejected the idea of many worlds. Early theologians like Hippolytus of Rome (c. 170–c. 235) and Philastrius (d. c. 397) thought that the atomists' position was a heresy.

The writings of Aristotle were lost to Western Europe for a long time, but when they were first translated into Latin they had a strong influence on Christian scholars of the time. Some of the most important are Albertus Magnus (1193–1280) and Thomas Aquinas (1224–1274).

Both argued against the idea that there could be more than one world.

A notable exception to the church's rejection of the idea is Nicholas of Cusa (1401–1464). In 1440, about the same time he became a priest, his most famous work, *De docta ignorantia (On Learned Ignorance)*, was published. He not only considered that Earth is not the only world in existence and that there could be life on other planets, he also believed that Earth moves, breaking with the traditional doctrine that Earth is the unmoving center of the universe.

Nicholas of Cusa went on to become a cardinal and a bishop, so his radical views did not cause any problems for him, which seems surprising considering the church's treatment of those who followed in his footsteps.

Nicolaus Copernicus (1473–1543) advanced the idea that Earth is not the center of the universe and that it revolves around the Sun. His universe theory was published shortly before his death and was later banned by the church.

Italian philosopher Giordano Bruno (1548–1600), a proponent of Copernicus's heliocentric theory who also argued that the Sun is just one star among many and that there might be inhabited planets orbiting those other stars, was burned at the stake as a heretic.

THE AGE OF THE TELESCOPE

The invention of the telescope in the early seventeeth century in the Netherlands had a huge impact on astronomy. Before that, all observations were limited to what could be seen with the naked eye. Now, telescopes allowed scientists to study celestial bodies in greater detail. Previously, the existence of life on other planets had been solely a matter of philosophical speculation. The magnification made possible by telescopes seemed to move the actual observation of extraterrestrial life into the realm of possibility.

The first to use the newly invented device to study celestial bodies was Italian astronomer and mathematician Galileo Galilei (1564–1642), who designed his own telescope in 1609 after hearing about the concept. Among other things, he discovered four of Jupiter's moons and he pub-

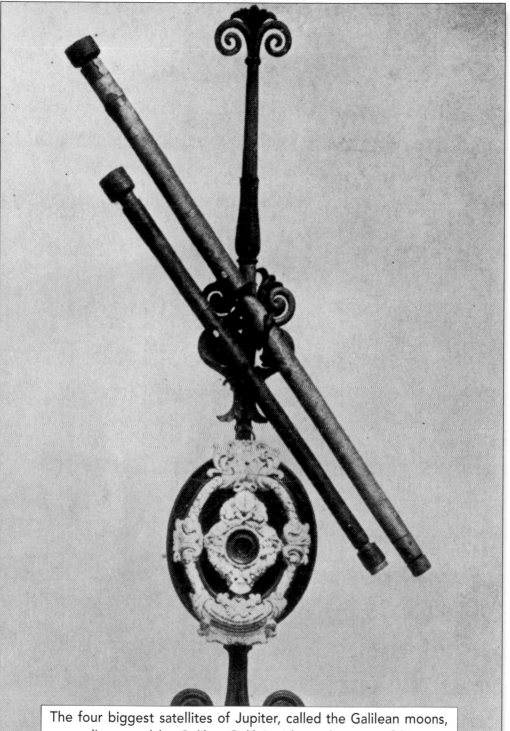

The four biggest satellites of Jupiter, called the Galilean moons, were discovered by Galileo Galilei with a telescope of his own design.

lished a book in 1632 titled *Dialogue Concerning the Two Chief World Systems, Ptolemaic and Copernican*, in which he supported the Copernican model. Since the church considered this a heresy, he was placed under house arrest. He was uncertain if life on the moon or other planets was possible, though. He had observed the moon closely and discovered that it was similar to Earth with its mountains and valleys, but since he did not believe that it was composed of earth and water, he concluded that the moon could not support life like on Earth.

By contrast, German astronomer Johannes Kepler (1571–1630), who developed three laws of planetary motion, speculated that there was life on Jupiter and on the moon. He even wrote what some consider to be the first work of science fiction, called *Somnium* (Latin for "Dream"), in which he tells the story of a journey to the moon, describing its geography as well as its inhabitants.

While Kepler's story fell into obscurity for centuries, the idea of the existence of extraterrestrial life became popular through the writings

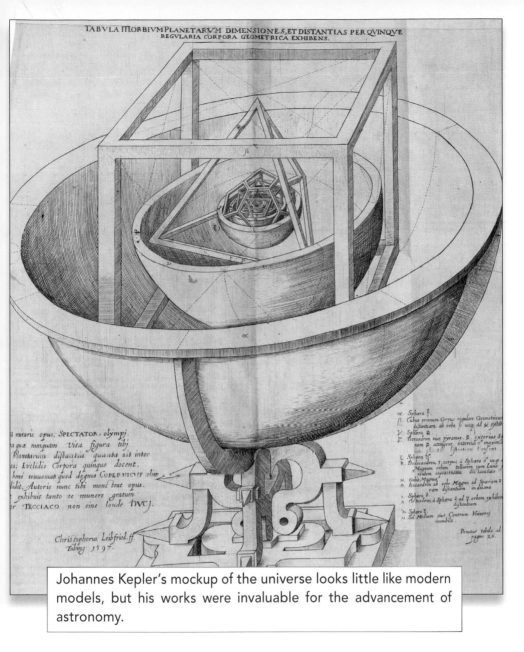

Johannes Kepler's mockup of the universe looks little like modern
models, but his works were invaluable for the advancement of
astronomy.

of French writer Bernard le Bovier de Fontenelle
(1657–1757) and Dutch scientist Christiaan
Huygens (1629–1695). Fontenelle's *Entretiens*

sur la pluralité des mondes (Conversations on the Plurality of Worlds) was soon translated into all major European languages after first being published in 1686, and the book went through about a hundred editions. Huygens's *The Celestial Worlds Discover'd: or, Conjectures Concerning the Inhabitants, Plants and Productions of the Worlds in the Planets*, published after his death in 1698, went into great detail on what he expected life on other worlds to look like.

William Herschel (1738–1822), whose observation of Uranus led to it being recognized as a planet, the first planet to be discovered in our solar system since ancient times, was convinced there was life on the moon. After observing Earth's satellite extensively, he believed he had discovered vegetation on the moon, and according to him, the craters were buildings constructed by intelligent inhabitants.

ESTABLISHING CONTACT

Despite the increasing quality of observation tools, astronomers were unable to provide an answer to whether there was life on the celestial bodies they were observing or not. The matter was widely discussed among the intellectuals of the eighteenth and nineteenth centuries.

The first to suggest trying to communicate with extraterrestrials was German mathematician Carl Friedrich Gauss (1777–1855), who proposed using a heliotrope, an instrument reflecting sunlight he had invented for land surveying purposes, to send signals of amplified light to the moon. He is also credited with the proposition to cut a right triangle into the Siberian forest and plant wheat inside it. The idea was that the contrast would make this construct visible from the moon or Mars, showing any observers that there were intelligent beings on Earth. Austrian astronomer Joseph Johann von Littrow (1781–1840) came up with the idea of filling a big circular canal with kerosene and lighting it at night. None of these suggestions were put into practice, though.

Several other people suggested the use of different forms of light signals over the course of the following century, but it was a new technology that became essential for humanity's attempts to find and communicate with extra-terrestrials: radio. The wireless transmission of signals proved to be a great way to communicate over large distances on Earth, so why not use it to communicate with other planets? Two of the pioneers of this technology were convinced that they had done exactly that.

Serbian-American inventor Nikola Tesla (1856–1943), best known for introducing the use of alternating current, claimed in an article published in 1901 that he had received radio communications from Mars while experimenting with a transmitting tower he had built in Colorado Springs. In his article "Talking with the Planets," he described rhythmic signals he observed that he was certain were not accidental or caused by any disturbances known to him, so he assumed they were intelligently controlled and intentionally transmitted from Mars or Venus. It is now believed that what Tesla observed were electromagnetic waves caused by lightning.

Guglielmo Marconi (1874–1937), often credited as the inventor of the radio although Tesla

In addition to the tower in Colorado Springs, Tesla later built another one in Shoreham, New York, the so-called Wardenclyffe Tower, to experiment with wireless transmission.

THE WAR OF THE WORLDS

Radio played a big part when Martians invaded Earth, but only as an entertainment medium. Orson Welles's adaptation of H. G. Wells's novel *The War of the Worlds* as a radio drama, which first aired on October 30, 1938, confused people who believed the fake news bulletins that Earth was under attack by Martians.

The broadcast was very realistic. Welles had changed the location and time of the story from Victorian England to the New Jersey of his day. Some listeners who missed the introduction were unable to tell that it was an entertainment program. Allegedly, the fictional reports that the U.S. Army was engaged in a fight with alien machines discharging poison gas and that New York was being evacuated caused mass hysteria and panic across the nation. At least that is what newspapers reported the next day, although it is now believed that the reaction was not as extreme as the reports suggest. Apparently the program caused only smaller, isolated incidents, because only relatively few people listened to it, and fewer still believed it was real.

While the mass panic in reaction to *The War of the Worlds* might be a myth, one can only wonder what effect it would have if we found proof of the existence of extraterrestrial life.

had beat him to it, conducted experiments in the 1920s to pick up radio signals from Mars. In 1924, when Mars and Earth were particularly close to each other in their orbits, even the U.S. Army joined in.

There is no evidence that any signals received were of extraterrestrial origin, though. It seems unlikely that Tesla or Marconi could have had success with the technology available to them, as the frequencies used were too low to penetrate Earth's ionosphere.

Radio astronomy started in earnest in the 1930s, when Karl Guthe Jansky (1905–1950) discovered natural radio emissions that came from the Milky Way while searching for a source of interference affecting transatlantic radiotelephone calls, and Grote Reber (1911–2002) built a parabolic radio telescope in his backyard that allowed him to detect a dozen more natural sources of radio emissions and produce a first radio map of the Milky Way.

CHAPTER TWO

ENTERING THE SPACE AGE

The bitter rivalry between the United States and the Soviet Union that dominated world politics for decades after the end of World War II brought space into focus for the superpowers. Crossing the final frontier was a way to upstage the rival power, and for humans to be able to leave Earth allowed for a new perspective on our planet and opened up new ways of exploring the universe. To echo the words of Neil Armstrong when he became the first person in history to set foot on the moon, it was a giant leap for mankind.

It is no coincidence that the search for extraterrestrial life intensified at a time when space was attracting attention like never before.

THE SEARCH BEGINS

In 1959, Giuseppe Cocconi and Philip Morrison, two physicists from Cornell University, published a short paper in the journal *Nature* titled "Searching for Interstellar Communication." It is generally thought of as the starting point of the modern search for extraterrestrial intelligence (SETI).

In their article, Cocconi and Morrison suggested looking for radio beacons from extraterrestrial civilizations, which existing radio telescopes were theoretically capable of detecting. Radio waves have a wide range of different frequencies, though, and trying to monitor them all would be impractical. So Cocconi and Morrison asked themselves at what frequency it would be most prudent to look. Their answer was 1420 megahertz. Natural hydrogen produces static at this frequency. Since hydrogen is the most abundant chemical element in the universe, it is rather noticeable. That could lead advanced civilizations to choose this frequency for sending beacons as younger civilizations might already

A NEW FRONTIER

From the 1960s onward, humanity searched for messages from extraterrestrial civilizations sent by radio waves.

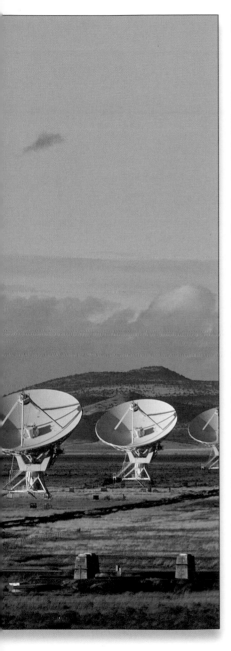

be paying attention to it.

How much that particular frequency suggested itself became clear the following year when Frank Drake, without having read Cocconi's and Morrison's article, came to the same conclusion. The young astronomer working at the National Radio Astronomy Observatory (NRAO) was the first to put this concept of searching for signals from extraterrestrial civilizations into practice.

Drake called his undertaking Project Ozma, named after Princess Ozma from L. Frank Baum's Oz series of books. The novels describe fantastical lands and their strange inhabitants. Drake hoped to find evidence of an extraterrestrial civilization on another planet, so the name is fitting.

The targets for his search were two sunlike stars roughly ten light-years from Earth, Tau Ceti and Epsilon Eridani. Starting in April 1960, Drake was able to use the NRAO's radio telescope in Green Bank, West Virginia, for two hundred hours. While it did not pick up any alien signals, his search attracted a lot of interest and has been emulated many times.

In 1961, the first scientific conference devoted to SETI took place at the Green Bank facility. While it was a small affair with only ten participants, there were great minds among them. One of the attendees, chemist Melvin Calvin, received the call that he had won the Nobel Prize while at the conference. The most influential result of the conference for the search for extraterrestrial intelligence was a tool devised by Frank Drake to estimate the number of communicating extraterrestrial civilizations in our galaxy, the Drake Equation.

THE DRAKE EQUATION

The Drake Equation is a formula written in 1961 by SETI pioneer Frank Drake to estimate the number of communicating (and therefore detectable) extraterrestrial civilizations and assess our chances of finding extraterrestrial life. To calculate the number of civilizations, Drake suggested multiplying several variables.

These variables are the average rate of new stars forming, the fraction of star systems that have planets, the number of planets per star system that could potentially support life, the fraction of these planets where life actually develops, the fraction of these planets where intelligent life develops, the fraction of these planets where a civilization emerges that produces signs of its existence we could detect, and the length of time such civilizations produce detectable signs. You can find the Drake Equation in the website links at the back of this book.

The problem with the Drake Equation is that we do not know the values of the variables, and with so many multipliers, small changes in the variables have a big impact on the result. The original estimates made at the conference lay between a thousand and a hundred million.

The Drake Equation is speculative and can only provide us with a rough estimate, but Frank Drake came up with it mainly to get people talking about the search for extraterrestrial intelligence, which it has done now for over fifty years.

FALSE ALARMS

It was not only scientists in America who were trying to find extraterrestrials, though. Several attempts to observe signals were undertaken in the Soviet Union in the 1960s, and at one point, the Soviets were convinced that they had discovered an alien beacon.

In 1963, Nikolai Kardashev proposed that a powerful source of radio waves designated as CTA-102 could be a sign of an extraterrestrial civilization. Gennady Sholomitskii called in a press conference in April 1965 to announce his findings that the emission varied in intensity following a regular pattern. In his and Kardashev's interpretation, this was proof that it was a broadcast from an advanced civilization. But later that year CTA-102 was identified as a quasar by American scientists.

In 1967, Jocelyn Bell, a Ph.D. student at the University of Cambridge, England, observed unusual signals while working on a project designed to study fluctuations in the intensity of compact radio waves, also known

Quasi-stellar radio sources, or quasars, confused researchers with their emission of electromagnetic energy. We now know the signals come from supermassive black holes.

as interplanetary scintillation. These pulses came at a regular interval and that caused her to call her supervisor, Antony Hewish, who was convinced that it must be a man-made signal. Further observation made clear that the pulses came from space, but the signal still looked like it was of artificial origin.

The source of the signal was called LGM-1, short for Little Green Men. But when similar sources were observed it became less and less likely that extraterrestrials were behind them.

THE WOW! SIGNAL

On August 15, 1977, the Big Ear Radio Observatory at Ohio State University picked up a seventy-two-second-long transmission that caused astronomer Jerry R. Ehman in his excitement to write "Wow!" on the printout of what he had spotted. Hence the name Wow! signal.

What was remarkable about the signal was that it was thirty times stronger than the background noise. And it was heard only on one of the telescope's fifty radio channels near the hydrogen line at 1420 MHz, which points to it being an artificial signal rather than a natural emission. That frequency is reserved for the purposes of radio astronomy, though, which makes it unlikely that the signal came from Earth. The way the signal rose and fell in intensity suggested movement, as would be expected from a transmission from space, but all known satellites and spacecraft could be ruled out as possible points of origin.

Since the signal was never observed again, it is difficult to assess its importance. It is possible that it came from an extraterrestrial civilization, but it is also possible that it was a transmission from Earth bouncing off a piece of space debris.

Instead of an alien civilization, they had dis-covered pulsating radio stars, pulsars for short, for which Hewish was awarded the Nobel Prize in 1974. The prize was shared with radio astron-omer Martin Ryle, but not with his student Joce-lyn Bell, leading to the award sometimes being referred to as the "No-Bell Prize" by those crit-ical of this decision.

THE SEARCH AT NASA

In 1971, there was a study conducted at NASA's Ames Research Center in collaboration with Stanford University and the American Society for Engineering Education to determine what the best possible system for picking up signals from space would look like. The answer was Project Cyclops.

Named after the race of one-eyed giants from Greek mythology, this Cyclops was sup-posed to be an array of dish antennas, each roughly 100 meters (109 yards) in size, covering a collecting area of 10 square kilometers (3.9 square miles), which would make it possible to pick up weak signals even from a great distance.

While this would eventually require about a thousand dishes, these were not necessary for the array to work. Smaller numbers of dishes could have been put to use right away. By gradually adding more, the estimated cost of $6 billion to $10 billion could have been spread over many years.

Bernard M. "Barney" Oliver was vice president for research at Hewlett Packard but had taken an interest in the search for extraterrestrial intelligence as early as 1960. He pointed out that bringing Project Cyclops into being would only

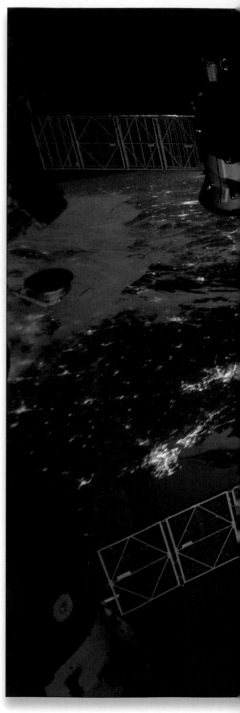

Considering the space agency's accomplishments, the involvement of NASA promised great things for the search for extraterrestrial intelligence.

cost as much as the United States spent on carrying on the war in Vietnam for three months. It is clear where the priorities lay as Project Cyclops was never built.

Nevertheless, NASA got involved in the search for extraterrestrial intelligence, although with considerably less money. In 1975, NASA started funding SETI design studies chaired by SETI pioneer Philip Morrison. The following year, theoretical SETI work was started at Ames Research Center and NASA's Jet Propulsion Laboratory (JPL) in La Cañada Flintridge, California.

Even though the funding was low, these programs were criticized by politicians who considered searching for life in the universe a waste of money, and Senator William Proxmire managed to stop the funding for 1982.

Astronomer Carl Sagan had been the youngest of the participants of the first SETI conference in 1961. He had since become widely known because of his endeavor to popularize science (millions of people watched the documentary TV series *Cosmos: A Personal Voyage* broadcast by PBS, which was presented by Sagan).

The way the search for extraterrestrial intelligence has been treated by politicians has caused some to question if the government even considers it an important matter.

Sagan was able to convince the senator that the scientific prospects of the programs were worth spending the taxpayers' money, though, and they were funded again in 1983.

After years of preparation, NASA's biggest effort started in 1992, on the five-hundred-year anniversary of Columbus reaching the New World, a date chosen for its symbolism because the scientists involved hoped to make great new discoveries. Called High Resolution Microwave Survey (HRMS), the program consisted of two different search strategies. Nearby sunlike stars were picked for a targeted search for promising signals. Also, a sky survey was supposed to keep an eye out for emissions originating from other points that were not specifically chosen for being looked at more closely.

HRMS received an annual budget of $12 million and was supposed to run over a span of ten years. This constituted a far more thorough search for extraterrestrial intelligence than any attempts undertaken before. But the U.S. Congress cancelled the funding after just one year in order to reduce the government budget deficit, saving every U.S. citizen roughly a nickel per year.

CHAPTER THREE

THE CURRENT SEARCH FOR EXTRATERRESTRIAL INTELLIGENCE

The untimely termination of the High Resolution Microwave Survey was a big setback for the search for extraterrestrial intelligence, but all was not lost when NASA had to put an end to its efforts. While government funding proved unreliable because it was easy to disparage the scientific effort to find extraterrestrial intelligence as a waste of money, privately funded projects were able to pick up the slack.

RISING FROM THE ASHES

The SETI Institute is a nonprofit organization originally founded in 1984. It had worked with NASA for several years developing the technology for the High Resolution Micro-wave Survey. The institute was able to raise money from private donors to carry on at least the targeted search. Barney Oliver, who had joined NASA and became part of the SETI Institute after its cancellation of the search, was able to convince his affluent acquaintances from the technology industry to provide the funding so that the search could continue.

Jill Tarter worked as project scientist for NASA's HRMS, and she was the director of Project Phoenix, before becoming the director of the SETI Institute's Center for SETI Research in 1999.

Project Phoenix, born like the mythological bird from the ashes of its predecessor, began its work in February 1995. It used the special equipment developed for NASA's HRMS, thanks to a long-term loan. By renting eleven thousand hours of observation time on radio telescopes around the world over the span of ten years, Project Phoenix was able to monitor about a thousand stars up to 250 light-years from Earth. It scanned tens of millions of very narrow channels for signals pointing to the existence of extraterrestrials. Of the more than one million observed signals, none was considered to have come from an alien species, though.

In 1996, the SETI League, a nonprofit organization founded in 1994, started Project Argus, an attempt to bring NASA's planned sky survey to life as well. In Greek mythology, Argus was a giant who never slept, with a hundred eyes that allowed him to see in every direction. This made him the ultimate watchman, a quality the project aimed to emulate.

Unlike earlier SETI programs, Project Argus does not rely on the big radio telescopes usually used in research. Instead, it employs small amateur radio telescopes that the members of the SETI League finance and operate themselves and which, unlike the big telescopes, are permanently devoted to the search for extraterrestrial intelligence.

Argus started with only five telescopes. But by November 2000, there were one hundred, the same number as the eyes of the project's namesake. Ten years later the number was close to 150. Fewer people got involved than the SETI League had hoped, though, as the original goal was to reach five thousand radio telescopes. This would allow

While a big radio telescope is not always available for SETI programs, arrays of smaller dishes like the Allen Telescope Array are a viable alternative.

the network to observe all directions at once.

Three years after launching Project Argus, the SETI League started planning Array 2K, an array of satellite TV dishes. It was supposed to be added to Project Argus but did not make it beyond a small-scale prototype because of lack of funding.

The SETI Institute was more successful in collecting the money for a similar project, the Allen Telescope Array in Hat Creek, California. It was named after Paul Allen, cofounder of Microsoft, who donated more than $30 million to make it become reality.

The Allen Telescope Array is a collection of small dishes that has a wider view of focus than existing telescopes and can change frequencies more easily. The first phase of the project with 42 working antennas was completed in 2007, but it is planned eventually to have 350. Because of a lack of funding, the Allen Array shut down between April and November of 2011 but has been able to operate since then. Dedicated to SETI 24/7, the array is surveying 4×10^{10} billion stars for powerful signals in the frequency range from 1420 MHz to 1720 MHz as well as examining a million stars at a broader range of frequencies.

SERENDIP

The University of California, Berkeley, has an ongoing program called the Search for Extra-terrestrial Radio Emissions from Nearby Developed Intelligent Populations, or SERENDIP for short. Unlike the projects run by the SETI Institute, SERENDIP does not make use of a tele-scope or an array that is dedicated to the search for extraterrestrial intelligence full-time. Instead it runs alongside other astronomical observation programs not concerned with SETI. This means that those other programs determine which part of the sky is observed. It may sound like a considerable drawback, but the upside to piggybacking on other programs is that SER-ENDIP can collect vast amounts of data without having to rent or build its own telescope.

Since 1980, there have been different incarnations of SERENDIP. The latest version, SERENDIP

The Arecibo Observatory in Puerto Rico is the biggest single-dish radio telescope in the world, and thanks to SERENDIP the data it collects is used in the search for extraterrestrials.

V, was installed at the Arecibo Observatory in Puerto Rico in 2009 and is capable of scanning over two billion channels, covering a bandwidth of 300 MHz, compared to the 168 million channels and 100 MHz bandwidth of its predecessor that operated from 1997 to 2006. The search for extraterrestrial intelligence is getting rapidly more effective, with continuing improvement.

SETI IN EUROPE

Not counting the early searches in Russia, there have been few attempts undertaken in Europe to find alien signals. The European countries have

SETI@HOME

Originally launched in May 1999, SETI@home is a computing project hosted by the University of California–Berkeley that allows volunteers to participate in the search for signals from space by donating a bit of computer power.

SETI programs need a lot of process time to analyze the data from the telescope, which is usually done by a supercomputer. These are expensive, though, and still only able to analyze the data somewhat superficially. because of their limited power. Researchers from UC Berkeley came up with a different solution: using computers in homes and offices, connected through the Internet, while they otherwise would be sitting around doing nothing.

The program works either as a screensaver or continuously in the background without inconveniencing the user. Each participating computer is sent a tiny amount of the data to process and transfers the results back to the database at UC Berkeley.

Combined, the network can analyze a huge amount of data. Already millions of people have participated, and there are teams of users and rankings to see who contributed the most. The competitive aspect is understandable, considering the person whose computer first detects a signal from an extraterrestrial civilization will probably go down in history.

shown little interest in the search for extraterrestrial intelligence, with Italy being the notable exception.

The Instituto di Radioastronomia in Bologna is cooperating with UC Berkeley and has been using the SERENDIP IV technology at the Medicina Radio Telescope since 1998 for SETI Italia. The parabolic antenna with a diameter of 32 meters (105 feet) is small compared to the 305 meter (1,001 foot) dish at Arecibo, but

The Medicina Radio Telescope in Italy is one of the few places in Europe where a search for extraterrestrial intelligence has been conducted for an extended amount of time.

there are plans to make use of one of the biggest telescopes in Europe, the Northern Cross, a T-shaped array consisting of 5,632 dipole antennas with a collecting area of 30,000 square meters (35,880 square yards), which may in the future be converted into a Square Kilometre Array (SKA) with a collecting area of—as the name implies—roughly one 1 kilometer (0.39 square miles). Additionally, the Sardinia Radio Telescope, a 64 meter (210 foot) parabolic dish completed in 2011 near San Basilio in Sardinia, could also be used. As it stands, SETI Italia is examining twenty-four million channels in the bands at 1.4–1.6 GHz, 4.8–6.5 GHz, 8.5 GHz, and 22–23.5 GHz, so far without finding any evidence of extraterrestrial signals.

A new way of searching for alien civilizations is made possible by LOFAR, the Low Frequency Array. Planned by the Netherlands Institute for Radio Astronomy (ASTRON), LOFAR is a gigantic array of ultimately about twenty-five thousand antennas. It is spread over forty-eight stations, most of which are located in the Netherlands. However, some are spread out (in Germany, France, Sweden, and England). This increases the array's capabilities considerably.

Additional remote stations may be created in Italy, Poland, Austria, and the Ukraine in the future as the array can be expanded without a problem. All of these stations are connected to

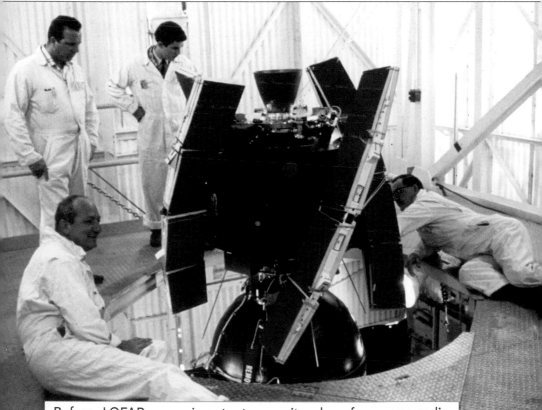

Before LOFAR, experiments to monitor low frequency radio signals had to be carried out in space with satellites like Explorer 38 and Explorer 49.

one of the most powerful supercomputers in Europe at the University of Groningen to analyze the collected data. The first parts of the array went online in 2010, and regular observations started two years later.

Because of its size, LOFAR can observe large parts of the sky, or even conduct several science projects at once. Its main use is to study the early history and evolution of the universe, since the array makes it possible to receive signals that are billions of years old. It can also scan low-frequency radio waves in the range of 30–80 MHz and 120–240 MHz for extraterrestrial signals. This helps other SETI projects that are focused on higher frequencies where there is less terrestrial interference.

Observing these lower frequencies is difficult because they are noisier. Some of our own TV and radio broadcasts fall into the bands covered by LOFAR. Filtering potential alien signals from the background noise is challenging, considering we do not even know what they might look like. Getting telescope time for SETI purposes has been difficult for the scientists pursuing it, but a piggyback search may be possible in the future.

OPTICAL SETI

When the search for extraterrestrial intelligence started, radio broadcasts were considered to be the most likely signals because it was thought that an interstellar broadcast with radio waves would require less energy—and therefore be less expensive—than an optical signal. Over the last twenty years, though, optical SETI has been given a lot more consideration.

The first laser was built in 1960, the same year Frank Drake conducted his pioneering SETI experiment. Soon after, a short-pulsed laser was suggested as a viable means of interstellar communication, although lasers at the time were not nearly powerful enough.

Modern lasers can outshine the sun for extremely brief periods of time. Since we are capable of building these, other civilizations may be able to as well. In the optical spectrum there is no terrestrial interference. Since the energy is

Using a laser for transmitting optical signals as a means of interstellar communication is now considered a viable alternative to radio waves.

focused into a very narrow beam, a laser can be observed from great distances with telescopes much smaller than those used in radio astronomy.

For such a signal to be detectable, though, it would have to be directed straight at our solar system. And unlike radio waves, light waves are absorbed by dust particles in space. This is why communication using optical signals would work only up to a distance of a thousand light-years. That may not be much compared to the size of the Milky Way, which has a diameter at least a hundred times that, but there still are millions of stars within a thousand light-years of Earth.

Programs for targeted searches were started at Harvard University in 1998 and at UC Berkeley the following year. The first optical telescope dedicated entirely to the search for extraterrestrial signals started its watch in 2006 at the Oak Ridge Observatory in Massachusetts. Funded by the Planetary Society and operated by a team from Harvard, the All-Sky Optical SETI telescope conducts sky surveys, going through a terabit of information per second in its search for laser pulses from alien civilizations.

CHAPTER FOUR

SEARCHING CLOSE TO HOME

The search for extraterrestrial intelligence has been the focus so far, but we are not only looking for intelligent beings. Even though getting in contact with an advanced civilization would be particularly exciting, detecting any sign of extraterrestrial life, even the smallest microorganism, would be one of the greatest discoveries in human history.

The reason why so much of the search is geared toward finding intelligent species is a practical one: we expect that advanced civilizations are detectable over large distances because of their use of technology, whereas you have to get really close to find living things not using technology. Taking Earth as (the only available) example, an observer could detect the presence of humans from light-years away thanks to the signals we constantly beam into space. To notice the presence of plants and animals, even those we consider to be intelligent, an observer would have to come much closer, into orbit or even to the surface of the planet.

Or at least that is true for an observer with our level of technology. This is why our search for extraterrestrial life that is not intelligent and technologically advanced is restricted to our solar system. The field of study that concerns itself with the origin and distribution of life in the universe is called astrobiology.

PREREQUISITES FOR LIFE

There are several conditions that have to be met for life to be possible. There have to be organic molecules, which to our knowledge are fairly widespread in the universe. For chemical reactions between these organic molecules to be possible, there has to be a medium in which they are able to move, which could be a gas or a liquid.

MARS

JUPITE

EARTH

VENUS

MERCURY

While there are no advanced civilizations in the solar system other than our own, we might yet discover extraterrestrial life close to Earth.

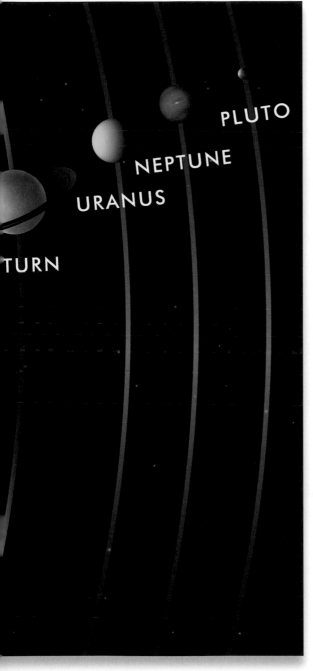

PLUTO

NEPTUNE

URANUS

TURN

Other candidates, like ammonia, methane, and ethane, have been considered. It is conceivable that they could support life, but liquid water offers the best conditions. The range of temperatures at which it stays liquid is wider. It is also higher—the boiling temperatures of ammonia, methane, and ethane are well below 0 degrees Celsius (32 degrees Fahrenheit)—which encourages chemical reactions. For a long time it was believed that water was rare outside of Earth, but recent efforts to explore our solar system have found water in a surprising number of places.

Finally there has to be a source of energy that fuels the life processes of organisms. This can be sunlight, but there are microbes living deep in the ocean on Earth that derive energy from chemical reactions instead. Therefore it can be concluded that life does not necessarily need to exist on a planet's (or moon's) surface but could flourish underground, and further from the sun than previously thought possible.

MARS

By now we know that there are no little green men living on Mars. The features that led earlier observers to believe that there was life on the Red Planet—vegetation, allegedly artificial canals, the famous "Face on Mars"—were misunderstandings caused by optical illusions.

Nonetheless, Mars remains one of the prime targets in our search for life in our solar system.

The *Curiosity* rover discovered that there once was flowing water as well as a freshwater lake on Mars. Its atmospheric pressure is too low to hold liquid water on the surface now but there could be evidence of past life. Additionally, there could still be liquid water underground where life could possibly exist.

Since landing on Mars in 2012, *Curiosity* has made exciting discoveries, including information suggesting that parts of the Red Planet may once have been habitable.

NASA's Viking landers, the first spacecraft to land successfully on Mars in 1976, were sent to the Red Planet for the express purpose of searching for life but did not find clear evidence of living microorganisms near their landing sites. However, this is still cause for debate. Some scientists argue that they did detect signs of life after all, while others claim that the equipment used was not sensitive enough to detect life even if it was there.

The European Space Agency (ESA) and the Russian Federal Space Agency plan to settle the question once and for all with their ExoMars (Exobiology on Mars) mission with launches in 2016 and 2018 and by a lander capable of detecting signs of past or present life to the Martian surface in January 2019.

THE MOONS OF JUPITER

Of the sixty-seven confirmed moons of Jupiter, two seem good candidates for harboring life: Io and Europa.

The unmanned probe *Galileo* collected data on Europa in eleven flybys and revealed that it is covered with a crust of water ice. The fractures observed in this icy crust are moving, which suggests tectonic or volcanic activity. The heat generated by this activity could mean that there is an ocean of liquid water underneath the

Pictures taken by *Voyager 1* show volcanic activity on Jupiter's moon Io, which makes it a possible candidate for supporting life.

crust where life could exist. Observations made with the Hubble Space Telescope in 2012 indicated that there might be jets of water bursting through the surface at the moon's south pole, possibly carrying signs of life from down below.

NASA has developed a mission concept for sending a spacecraft into Europa's orbit to examine its icy shell and analyze its atmosphere, which could provide definite proof of the existence of liquid water and particles contained in that water. The mission, which is supposed to launch in the 2020s, would perform forty-five flybys to collect data, going as low as 16 miles (25 km) above the surface.

The ESA is also planning a mission to explore Jupiter and its icy moons. Called JUICE (JUpiter ICy moons Explorer), the mission is planned to launch in 2022 and reach Jupiter by 2030, exploring the planet as well as its moons Europa, Ganymede, and Callisto, two other satellites that may have liquid oceans under their surface.

Io, Jupiter's third-largest moon, does not seem to have water in liquid or solid form,

There might be an ocean of liquid water under Europa's fractured crust, a potential habitat for simple life-forms.

and it is exposed to lethal radiation. Its atmosphere and volcanic activity still make it a possible candidate for life, although most likely life that existed a long time ago. If there still is life today, it exists far below the surface where it would be impossible to detect with our current technology.

THE MOONS OF SATURN

Saturn's sixth-largest moon, Enceladus, has a diameter of only 310 miles (500 km) but the small satellite is another hot candidate for harboring life as it shows conditions very similar to those on Europa.

From 2005 on, the *Cassini-Huygens* spacecraft observed geysers erupting at high speed on Enceladus, which carry ice and possibly liquid water (as well as various gases) from an underground sea to the surface. Traces of minerals, another important ingredient for potential habitability, have also been detected. *Cassini* passes Enceladus three more times in late 2015 to collect more data but there is no additional mission

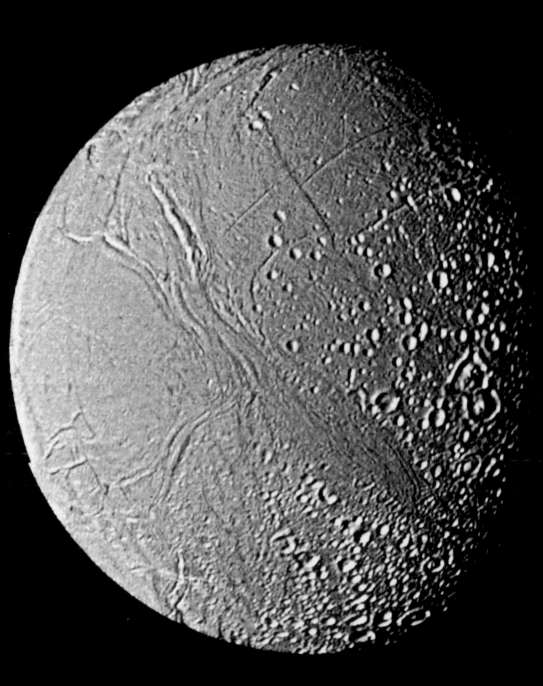

Enceladus, named after a giant from Greek mythology, is hardly a giant, with only 14 percent of the diameter of Earth's moon. Nonetheless, it might harbor life.

to the minute moon planned at this point.

Titan, Saturn's largest moon with ten times the diameter of Enceladus, has a chemically active atmosphere that could protect life from radiation, and there are liquid lakes of ethane and methane on its surface. Titan's temperature is a lot lower than the temperature on Earth, with an average of -179°C (-290°F). If there is life, it would be very different from what we know. But it is conceivable that there is life, and the presence of methane in Titan's atmosphere could be an indication of its existence, as methane is usually destroyed by sunlight. There is methane in the atmosphere of Earth because it is constantly emitted by the life on our planet, and the same could be true for Titan.

EARTH

Obviously there is life on our own planet, although cynics sometimes wonder if it is intelligent. There are some who claim that evidence of the existence of extraterrestrial life can be found right here, that aliens visited Earth in the

UFOS

The term "UFO," the abbreviation of "unidentified flying object," was coined in the early 1950s, after sightings of what were also called "flying discs" or "flying saucers" had increased in the years before, causing the U.S. Air Force to investigate. Some people thought these UFOs to be signs of extraterrestrials visiting Earth, and today the term is often used to refer to an extraterrestrial spacecraft, although there is no proof that UFOs are of extraterrestrial origin.

In fact, a vast majority of UFO sightings are easily explained by people mistaking planes, balloons, missile tests or other military experiments, meteors, or weather phenomena for ships from space (in the case of the U.S. Air Force's Project Blue Book about 94 percent of the 12,618 events investigated between 1952 and 1969 were classified as identified). While it is possible that some cases of UFO sightings that are not so readily explained were indeed encounters with alien spacecraft, there is no clear evidence to support this.

past and are still doing it today. Proponents of this position point to historical records and artifacts as alleged proof.

Monumental structures like the Great

Pyramids of Egypt or Stonehenge are taken as examples that humans of the time must have had help from outer space because they would not have been able to build them otherwise. Studies of the methods used by our ancestors have shown that they had no need for help from alien engineers, though.

Large designs of figures made on the ground that could only be seen in full from above like the 180 feet (55 m) high Cerne Abbas Giant in England or the Nazca Lines in Peru are sometimes considered to be attempts at communicating with visitors from space. More likely they

Crop circles have appeared frequently in the past few decades and are seen by some as a sign of visits from extraterrestrials.

are an expression of worship to be seen by the gods.

Elements of old paintings or written records that are thought by some to be flying saucers and alien visitors can as easily be explained as depictions of planets, comets, or meteorites.

Phenomena like crop circles and cattle mutilations are far more likely the result of terrestrial pranks than a sign of extraterrestrial visitors, and stories of alien abductions that often crop up in the tabloids are usually easily explained by sleep paralysis, which occurs sometimes when a person is about to fall asleep or waking up. This terrifying state of not being able to move for up to a few minutes can be accompanied by hallucinations. So far there have been no signs of extraterrestrials on Earth that held up to scientific scrutiny.

CHAPTER FIVE

THE FUTURE OF THE SEARCH

Despite funding being problematic at times for programs searching for extraterrestrial life, exobiological endeavors have come a long way since the early days of SETI. They may not have had a positive result, but with our increasing knowledge of the universe and improving technology it seems to be only a matter of time before evidence of life beyond Earth is discovered.

Also, future space missions and new approaches to SETI are under development to find the definitive answer to one of humanity's greatest and most exciting questions.

OCEAN WORLDS AND A DESERT PLANET

At the time of this writing, the budget proposal for NASA, $18.5 billion in total, includes not only $140 million for development of the mission to Europa, the launch date of which is set in the proposal as 2022, but an additional $86 million to start the Ocean Worlds Exploration Program. The focus of this program is the search for life on the moons of Jupiter and Saturn, particularly Titan and Enceladus.

Despite this new focus on ocean worlds, Mars

حول المدار
55 ساعة

يدخل المسبار مداره
حول المريخ

يبعد المدار
22,000

طئ المسبار لسرعة
14,000 كم/س
هيداً ل ال

For a long time, exploration of space was dominated by the United States and Russia, but others, such as the United Arab Emirates, are now planning missions of their own.

is still at the center of attention. In addition to the ESA's
ExoMars project to investigate the Red Planet further,
the United Arab Emirates
announced recently that it
intends to send a mission to
Mars as well.

Called Al Amal (Hope),
money is no object for this
mission because leaders see
it as an important investment.
With the goal of inspiring and
showing that the Emirates can
compete in the field of space
science, the project is supposed to finish in record time.

The launch is scheduled
for 2020, and if it goes as planned, the probe
will reach Mars in 2021, the fiftieth anniversary
of the Emirate's independence. The probe is
meant to study changes in the atmosphere,
which in light of the recent detection of methane on Mars could give information about life.

Establishing a colony on Mars would be another great leap for mankind, but for the time being it does not seem to be a realistic endeavour.

The most ambitious—and possibly the most unrealistic—mission that is supposed to go to the Red Planet is Mars One. This private space-flight project plans to send the first manned mission to Mars, establishing a permanent settlement there by 2025. Despite the lack of an option for a return flight to Earth, more than two hundred thousand people registered on the Mars One website to be considered. Only four will go on the first flight, with the colony projected to expand slowly with additional crews being sent over the course of the following decades.

But it seems doubtful that it will ever happen because of shaky funding and the dangers involved, which have drawn a lot of criticism. Astronauts on Mars could conduct more conclusive experiments than probes or landers, but a settlement on our neighboring planet is still out of reach. NASA has plans for a manned mission to Mars, though, which may be launched in the 2030s.

SETI IN SPACE

Bigger and better telescopes are built on Earth to observe the stars and maybe find signals from extraterrestrial civilizations, like the

Square Kilometre Array (SKA) in Australia and South Africa.

But a big step could be moving the search into space. A telescope on the far side of the moon that always faces away from Earth would be shielded from terrestrial interference, making it an ideal spot to search for alien signals. ASTRON is looking into the possibility of a Lunar LOFAR that could explore low frequencies that cannot be observed from Earth. But there are many costs and logistical problems involved.

The James Webb Space Telescope scheduled to launch in 2018 might be able to detect chemicals in the atmosphere of exoplanets that could indicate the presence of an advanced civilization.

Another possible option is making use of an effect known as gravitational microlensing. The gravity of a massive object like a star can be used to bend light like a lens and observe more distant objects that are directly in line with them. Using this method, hundreds of exoplanets have been discovered so far. By placing a telescope far out into space, the sun could

Astronomer Marc Postman, here standing next to a model of the James Webb Space Telescope, is one of the leading scientists working on space telescopes.

be used as a magnifying glass. This would make it possible to take a closer look at specific planets and even to send signals there.

Since bringing such a telescope into position would take hundreds of years given the currently available technology, this is a plan for the far future.

MESSAGE IN A BOTTLE

A different approach to contacting other civilizations that might be out there was taken in 1972 when *Pioneer 10* was launched. The main purpose of this space probe was to fly by and take

THE FERMI PARADOX

Enrico Fermi (1901–1954) was an Italian-born physicist, who became a U.S. citizen in 1944. He was awarded the Nobel Price in Physics in 1938. He is best known for his contributions to the field of nuclear physics, but he has had an impact on the search for extraterrestrial intelligence through a problem named after him: the Fermi Paradox.

The origin of the Fermi Paradox was a lunchtime conversation between Fermi and some of his colleagues at Los Alamos. They were discussing the possibility of the existence of alien societies and whether travel at above the speed of light was achievable. This led Fermi to ask the question: "Where is everybody?"

What seems like an innocent question at first has major implications for the search for extraterrestrial intelligence. Fermi concluded that any sufficiently advanced alien civilization would be able to spread all across the galaxy. It might take millions of years, which sounds like a lot, but since it is only a tiny fraction of the age of the galaxy (currently estimated at 13.82 billion years) it should be possible, assuming there are any alien societies out there.

Since we have not found any evidence of alien societies so far, even though they have had enough time to visit us or leave marks somehow, one could come to the conclusion that there aren't any. Those who are searching for extraterrestrial life have to come up with a different explanation when faced with Fermi's question.

pictures of Jupiter and its moons and collect data about the outer solar system. But since it would be the first man-made object to travel that far from Earth, it was decided that it should include a message.

A metal plaque with a message designed by Carl Sagan and Frank Drake was attached to the probe. The *Pioneer* plaque shows a picture of a man and a woman in front of a silhouette of the spacecraft (to indicate what size humans are), a schematic of our solar system, as well as the position of the sun relative to fourteen pulsars. A copy of this plaque was also attached to *Pioneer 11*, which launched in 1973.

Voyager 1 and *Voyager 2*, launched in 1977, also carried a message on board, the Golden Record. These 12-inch (30-cm) discs not only have a schematic representation of their origin on them, they also work as phonograph records.

Any species that finds them—and correctly interprets the included instructions for how the record can be played—will find 115 pictures showing what life on Earth looks like. There are

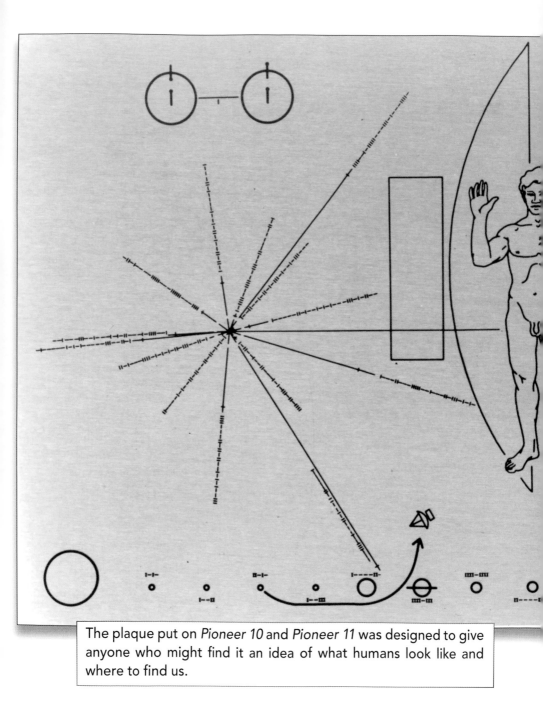

The plaque put on *Pioneer 10* and *Pioneer 11* was designed to give anyone who might find it an idea of what humans look like and where to find us.

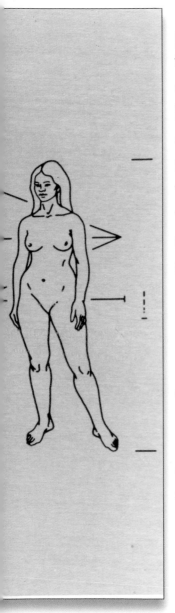

photos of people from all across the world, landscapes, examples of architecture, as well as a glimpse into our understanding of science. Additionally there are audio recordings, greetings spoken in fifty-five different languages, sounds from Earth (e.g., crickets and the sound of the wind), and ninety minutes of music.

These four spacecraft are the furthest man-made objects from Earth. *Voyager 1*, the most distant, left our solar system in 2012 and entered interstellar space. *Voyager 2*, 16 billion kilometers (10 billion miles) from Earth in 2015, is expected to cross into interstellar space in the near future. *Pioneer 10* and *Pioneer 11*, which unlike *Voyager 1* and *Voyager 2* are no longer communicating, will follow suit. Eventually they will pass other stars, but it will take a long time until that happens.

In forty thousand years, *Voyager 1* will come within 1.6 light-years of AC+79 3888, and *Voyager 2* will come within 1.7 light-years of Ross 248—a thousand times its current distance from the sun. These messages in a bottle are floating in an ocean of incredible size, and it seems unlikely that they will ever be read.

New Horizons, a space probe launched in 2006 to study Pluto, had a digital message streamed to it after it completed its primary mission in the summer of 2015. The fifth human spacecraft to leave the solar system will carry with it the One

Voyager 1, the man-made object that is the furthest away from its place of origin, has entered interstellar space, carrying greetings from Earth.

Earth Message. Unlike the messages on the *Pioneer* and *Voyager* probes, it was not put together by a small team of experts. Instead, it was crowd-sourced, created by a group of people, giving everybody the chance to contribute.

CALLING THE STARS

The so-called Arecibo Message has a better chance of being picked up because this powerful broadcast sent from the Arecibo Observatory in Puerto Rico in 1974 was aimed at globular star cluster Messier 13, which contains upward of three hundred thousand stars. The message was sent in the form of 1,679 binary digits—the ones and zeros of binary code were transmitted by shifting the frequency—and was less than three minutes long.

The message will take twenty-five thousand years to reach its intended target, and if an alien scientist engaged in the equivalent of our SETI happens to catch it, any answer will take just as long to get back to Earth. However, the Arecibo

Message breaks one of the golden rules established by our scientists: a signal has to repeat itself to be accepted as authentic. The Arecibo Message was sent only once, so even if somebody out there catches it, they might consider it nothing but a weird anomaly if they apply similar standards.

MAKING CONTACT

Some people find it unwise to send out messages that give away our whereabouts. After all we do not know what is out there. Maybe one of those messages will draw the attention of aggressive and hostile aliens. While that is possible, it is not much of an added risk. We are making our presence known anyway, since we are constantly broadcasting signals other civilizations could pick up, even though these signals are not meant to establish contact. Maybe there are alien species right now judging us by our television programs (although they would have to have receivers far more sensitive than the ones currently in use on Earth).

Stephen Hawking has done a lot to advance our understanding of the universe, so his words of warning concerning alien contact command attention.

Famed physicist Stephen Hawking has expressed his concern that a visit by aliens could have a negative impact on humanity. A visit seems unlikely, though, considering the vast interstellar distances. Even traveling close to the speed of light, such a voyage could take hundreds or thousands of years.

The same problem applies to two-way communication with an extraterrestrial civilization if we find a signal. Exchanging messages could take a lot longer than a human lifespan, and it might even be impossible to decipher any messages we receive.

Nonetheless, any confirmed signal from another civilization would be a monumental discovery, as would be the detection of the simplest form of extraterrestrial life. It is so monumental, in fact, that it is impossible to say what impact it would have. To know for sure that Earth is not the only place that can support life would mean that humanity would have to reconsider its place in the universe.

GLOSSARY

ARECIBO The second-largest radio telescope in the world, near the city of Arecibo, Puerto Rico.

ASTROBIOLOGY A field of study that concerns itself with life in the universe.

ATOMISM A natural philosophy whose followers believed that the cosmos consisted of tiny indestructible particles.

BANDWIDTH The frequency range in which a signal is transmitted.

DRAKE EQUATION An equation formulated by Frank Drake to estimate the number of extraterrestrial civilizations in our galaxy.

EXOBIOLOGY The study of extraterrestrial life (often used synonymously with astrobiology, although astrobiology includes life on Earth).

FERMI PARADOX A question by Enrico Fermi asking why humankind has not been contacted by any extraterrestrial civilization yet.

HELIOCENTRISM An astronomical model that places the sun at the center of the solar system, around which the planets revolve, as opposed to the geocentric model, which assumes Earth is at the center.

HERTZ The unit of frequency, defined as one cycle per second.

HRMS High Resolution Microwave Survey, a SETI program developed by NASA, which was cancelled in 1993 after only one year.

LIGHT-YEAR 5.87×10^{12} miles (9.46×10^{12} km), the distance light travels in a vacuum over the course of a year.

NASA The National Aeronautics and Space Administration of the United States.

OPTICAL SETI The search for extraterrestrial signals in the visible spectrum.

PLURALITY OF WORLDS The philosophical belief that there are planets other than Earth that may support life.

RADIO ASTRONOMY Using radio waves to explore the universe.

RADIO WAVES Electromagnetic radiation traveling at the speed of light, which can be used to transmit signals over long distances.

SERENDIP Search for Extraterrestrial Radio Emissions from Nearby Developed Intelligent

Populations, a SETI project run by the University of California, Berkeley.

SETI The search for extraterrestrial intelligence by looking for signals from alien civilizations.

TELESCOPE ARRAY An arrangement of a number of smaller antennas.

FOR MORE INFORMATION

Berkeley SETI Research Center
7 Gauss Way
Berkeley, CA 94720
(510) 642-4921
Website: https://seti.berkeley.edu

The SETI Research Center at UC Berkeley has several programs searching for extraterrestrial life, including SETI@home, through which people participating can donate computing power. The necessary software can be downloaded from the Research Center's website.

Canadian Space Agency (CSA)
John H. Chapman Space Centre
6767 Route de l'Aéroport
Saint-Hubert, QC J3Y 8Y9
Canada
(613) 998-2383
Website: http://www.asc-csa.gc.ca

The CSA, founded in 1989 with the mandate to advance the knowledge of space for the benefit of Canadians and humanity, cooperates closely with other space agencies like NASA and ESA.

European Space Agency (ESA)
ESA HQ Mario-Nikis
8-10 rue Mario Nikis

75738 Paris, France
Website: http://www.esa.int

Thanks to its twenty-two member states the European Space Agency, established in 1975, is able to conduct research in a way no European country could easily finance on its own. ESA's website provides a great overview of the agency's activities, including news of recent discoveries.

National Aeronautics and Space Administration (NASA)
NASA Headquarters
300 E Street SW, Suite 5R30
Washington, DC 20546
(202) 358-0001
Website: http://www.nasa.gov

Since being established by President Dwight D. Eisenhower in 1958, NASA has been at the forefront of space exploration. NASA's website offers a wealth of information on past, present, and future missions, as well as a section concerned with astrobiology (https://astrobiology.nasa.gov).

The Planetary Society
85 South Grand Avenue
Pasadena, CA 91105

(626) 793-5100

Website: http://www.planetary.org

The Planetary Society was cofounded in 1980 by Carl Sagan, Bruce Murray, and Louis Friedman with the intention to inspire a widespread interest in space exploration and educate the public about science. The nonprofit organization with more than forty thousand members worldwide sponsors projects developing new space technologies and searching for life in the universe.

SETI Institute

189 Bernardo Avenue, Suite 100

Mountain View, CA 94043

(650) 961-6633

Website: http://www.seti.org

A nonprofit organization founded in 1984, the SETI Institute has worked with NASA and even continued NASA's work when public funding for SETI efforts was cut. Thirty years after beginning operations, the SETI Institute employs 130 people to pursue its mission of exploring the nature of life in the universe.

SETI League

433 Liberty Street

Little Ferry, NJ 07643

(201) 641-1770

Website: http://www.setileague.org

The SETI League is a nonprofit organization originally founded in 1994. Its 1,500 members from all over the world are united in their goal to search for extraterrestrial intelligence using radio technology available to everyone, for which the league offers technical support.

WEBSITES

Because of the changing nature of Internet links, Rosen Publishing has developed an online list of websites related to the subject of this book. This site is updated regularly. Please use this link to access the list:

http://www.rosenlinks.com/SOE/New

FOR FURTHER READING

Billings, Lee. *Five Billion Years of Solitude. The Search for Life Among the Stars.* New York, NY: Current, 2013.

Catling, David Charles. *Astrobiology. A Very Short Introduction.* Oxford, England: Oxford University Press, 2013.

Davies, Paul. *The Eerie Silence: Renewing Our Search for Alien Intelligence.* Boston, MA: Houghton Mifflin Harcourt, 2010.

DeVito, Carl L. *Science, SETI, and Mathematics.* New York, NY: Berghahn, 2014.

Dick, Steven J. *The Impact of Discovering Life Beyond Earth.* Cambridge, England: Cambridge University Press, 2015.

Flynn, Mike. *Outer Space Explained.* New York, NY: Rosen Publishing, 2015.

Gray, Robert H. *The Elusive Wow. Searching for Extraterrestrial Intelligence.* Chicago, IL:

Palmer Square Press, 2011.

Impley, Chris. *The Living Cosmos. Our Search for Life in the Universe.* Cambridge, England: Cambridge University Press, 2011.

Irwin, Louis N., and Dirk Schulze-Makuch. *Cosmic Biology. How Life Could Evolve on Other Worlds.* New York, NY: Springer, 2011.

Kaufman, Marc. *First Contact. Scientific Breakthroughs in the Hunt for Life Beyond Earth.* New York, NY: Simon & Schuster, 2011.

Longstaff, Alan. *Astrobiology: An Introduction.* Boca Raton, FL: CRC Press, 2014.

Michaud, Michael A. *Contact with Alien Civilizations: Our Hopes and Fears About Encountering Extraterrestrials.* New York, NY: Copernicus Books, 2010.

Plaxco, Kevin W. *Astrobiology: A Brief*

Introduction. Baltimore, MD: Johns Hopkins University Press, 2011.

Seeds, Michael A., and Dana E. Backman. *Horizons. Exploring the Universe.* Pacific Grove, CA: Brooks/Cole, 2014.

Vakoch, Douglas A., ed. *Archaeology, Anthropology, and Interstellar Communication.* Washington, DC: NASA, 2012.

Vakoch, Douglas A., ed. *Astrobiology, History, and Society. Life Beyond Earth and the Impact of Discovery.* Berlin and Heidelberg, Germany: Springer, 2013.

Vakoch, Douglas A., ed. *Communication with Extraterrestrial Intelligence.* Albany, NY: State University of New York Press, 2011.

Vakoch, Douglas A., ed. *The Drake Equation. Estimating the Prevalence of Extraterrestrial Life Through the Ages.* Cambridge, England: Cambridge University Press, 2015.

Vakoch, Douglas A., ed. *Extraterrestrial Altruism. Evolution and Ethics in the Cosmos.* Berlin and Heidelberg, Germany: Springer, 2014.

Vakoch, Douglas A., and Albert A. Harrison, ed. *Civilizations Beyond Earth. Extraterrestrial Life and Society.* New York, NY: Berghahn Books, 2011.

BIBLIOGRAPHY

Anderson, Paul Scott. "35 Years Later, the 'Wow!' Signal Still Tantalizes." Universe Today, February 24, 2012. Retrieved June 12, 2015 (http://www.universetoday.com).

Bennett, Jeffrey, and Seth Shostak. *Life in the Universe*, 3rd ed. Boston, MA: Addison-Wesley, 2012.

Burnell, S. Jocelyn Bell. "Little Green Men, White Dwarfs or Pulsars?" Big Ear Radio Observatory, September 21, 2004. Retrieved June 12, 2015 (http://www.bigear.org/vol1no1/burnell.htm).

Choi, Charles Q. " Gigantic Radio Telescope to Search for First Stars and Galaxies." Space.com, January 30, 2012. Retrieved June 12, 2015 (http://www.space.com/14399-giant-lofar-radio-antennas-telescope.html).

Crowe, Michael J. *The Extraterrestrial Life Debate: Antiquity to 1915. A Source Book.* Notre Dame, IN: University of Notre Dame Press, 2008.

Dick, Steven J. *Life on Other Worlds. The 20th-Century Extraterrestrial Life Debate.* Cambridge, England: Cambridge University Press, 1998.

Garber, Stephen J. "Searching for Good Science. The Cancellation of NASA's SETI Program." *Journal of the British Interplanetary Society*, vol. 52, 1999, pp. 3–12.

Hoerner, Sebastian von. *SETI und das Leben im All.* Munich, Germany: Verlag C. H. Beck, 2003.

Lanxon, Nate. "SETI Founder Dr. Frank Drake Outlines Ambitious Plans." *Wired*, January 25, 2010. Retrieved June 12, 2015 (http://www.wired.co.uk).

Malek, Caline. " UAE's Mars Space Mission Has a New Name: Hope." *The National*, May 6, 2015. Retrieved June 12, 2015 (http://www.thenational.ae).

Montebugnoli, Stelio. "SETI in Italy." SETI
   Italia. Retrieved June 12, 2015 (http://www.
   seti-italia.cnr.it).

NASA. "The Pioneer Missions." Retrieved June
   12, 2015 (https://www.nasa.gov/centers/
   ames/missions/archive/pioneer.html).

NASA Jet Propulsion Laboratory. "Voyager.
   The Interstellar Mission." Retrieved June
   12, 2015 (http://voyager.jpl.nasa.gov/index.
   html).

SETI Institute. "The Drake Equation."
   Retrieved June 12, 2015 (http://www.seti.
   org/drakeequation).

SETI Institute. "SETI 101." Retrieved June 12,
   2015 (http://www.seti.org/node/662).

Shuch, H. Paul, ed. *Searching for Extraterres-
   trial Intelligence: SETI Past, Present, and
   Future.* Berlin and Heidelberg, Germany:
   Springer, 2011.

Stromberg, Joseph. "Where in the Solar System Are We Most Likely to Find Life?" *Smithsonian*, March 12, 2014. Retrieved June 12, 2015 (http://www.smithsonianmag.com).

Tesla, Nikola. "Talking with the Planets." United States Early Radio History. Retrieved June 12, 2015 (http://earlyradiohistory.us/1901talk.htm).

Wall, Mike. "Signs of Alien Life Will Be Found by 2025, NASA's Chief Scientist Predicts." Space.com, April 7, 2015. Retrieved June 12, 2015 (http://www.space.com/29041-alien-life-evidence-by-2025-nasa.html).

Webb, Stephen. *If the Universe Is Teeming with Aliens ... Where Is Everybody? Fifty Solutions to the Fermi Paradox and the Problem of Extraterrestrial Life.* New York, NY: Copernicus Books, 2002.

INDEX

E

Earth, search for extra-
terrestrial life on, 68,
70–72
Egyptian pyramids, 69
Ehman, Jerry R., 32
Enceladus, 66, 74
Europa, 62, 64, 74
European Space Agency
(ESA), 62, 64, 76
ExoMars mission, 62, 76
extraterrestrials, early
attempts at communi-
cation with, 18–20, 23

F

Fermi, Enrico, 82
Fermi Paradox, 82
Fontenelle, Bernard le
Bovier de, 17, 18

G

Galileo Galilei, 14–16
Galileo probe, 62
Ganymede, 64
Gauss, Carl Friedrich, 19
gravitational microlens-
ing, 79–81
Greece, theories of
extraterrestrial life in
ancient Greece, 7–12

H

Hawking, Stephen, 89
heliotrope, 19
Herschel, William, 18
Hewish, Antony, 31, 33
High Resolution Micro-
wave Survey (HRMS),
38, 39, 41
Hippolytus, 12
Hubble Space Telescope,
64
Huygens, Christiaan,
17–18

I

Instituto di Radioastronomia, 49
Io, 64–66
Italy, SETI projects in,
49–50

J

James Webb Space Tele-
scope, 79
Jansky, Karl Guthe, 23
Jet Propulsion
Laboratory, 36
Jupiter, search for life
on moons of, 62–66,
74, 81
JUICE, 64–66

ABOUT THE AUTHOR

Dr. Nicki Peter Petrikowski is a literary scholar as well as an editor, author, and translator. Since childhood he has been fascinated by the idea of extraterrestrial life, hoping that its discovery will bring humankind closer together.

PHOTO CREDITS